Art and Culture

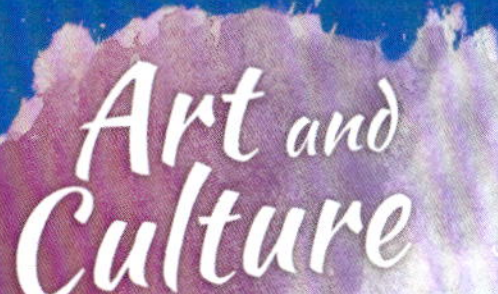

King's Cross

Partitioning Shapes

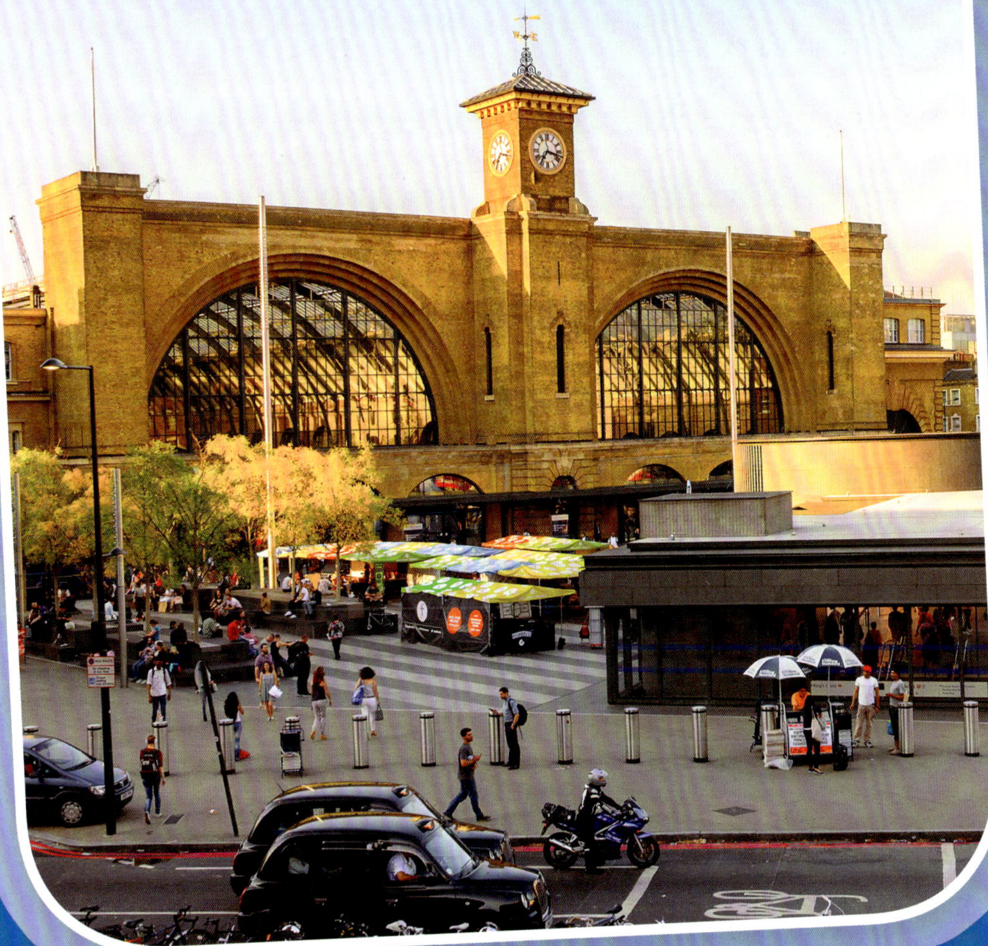

Dona Herweck Rice

Consultants

Colene Van Brunt
Math Coach
Hillsborough County Public Schools

Publishing Credits

Rachelle Cracchiolo, M.S.Ed., *Publisher*
Conni Medina, M.A.Ed., *Managing Editor*
Dona Herweck Rice, *Series Developer*
Emily R. Smith, M.A.Ed., *Series Developer*
Diana Kenney, M.A.Ed., NBCT, *Content Director*
June Kikuchi, *Content Director*
Susan Daddis, M.A.Ed., *Editor*
Karen Malaska, M.Ed., *Editor*
Kevin Panter, *Senior Graphic Designer*

Image Credits: front cover, p.1, p.16 Anton Ivanov/Shutterstock; back cover Chris Dorney/Shutterstock; pp.2–3 Daniel Tomlinson; p.5 (top) Gordon Bell/Shutterstock; p.5 (bottom) PhotoLondonUK; p.7 Guildhall Library & Art Gallery/Heritage Images/Getty Images; p8 Hulton Archive/Getty Images; p.10 Team Jackson; p.11 W.C. Johnston; p.13 (background) George Clerk; pp.14–15 SolarZebra/Shutterstock; p.17 Sergey Didenko/Shutterstock; p.18 pio3/Shutterstock; p.19 (top) Willy Barton/Shutterstock; p.19 (bottom) James Davidson; p.21 Yolanta/Shutterstock; p.23 Lucian Milasan/Shutterstock; all other images iStock and/or Shutterstock.

Library of Congress Cataloging-in-Publication Data

Names: Rice, Dona, author.
Title: Art and culture. King's Cross / Dona Herweck Rice.
Other titles: King's Cross
Description: Huntington Beach, CA : Teacher Created Materials, 2018. |
  Includes index. | Audience: K to Grade 3. |
Identifiers: LCCN 2017055028 (print) | LCCN 2017057208 (ebook) | ISBN
  9781480759886 (eBook) | ISBN 9781425856946 (pbk.)
Subjects: LCSH: King's Cross Station (London, England)--Juvenile literature.
Classification: LCC TF302.L6 (ebook) | LCC TF302.L6 R53 2018 (print) | DDC
  385.3/140942142--dc23
LC record available at https://lccn.loc.gov/2017055028

Teacher Created Materials

5301 Oceanus Drive
Huntington Beach, CA 92649-1030
www.tcmpub.com

ISBN 978-1-4258-5694-6

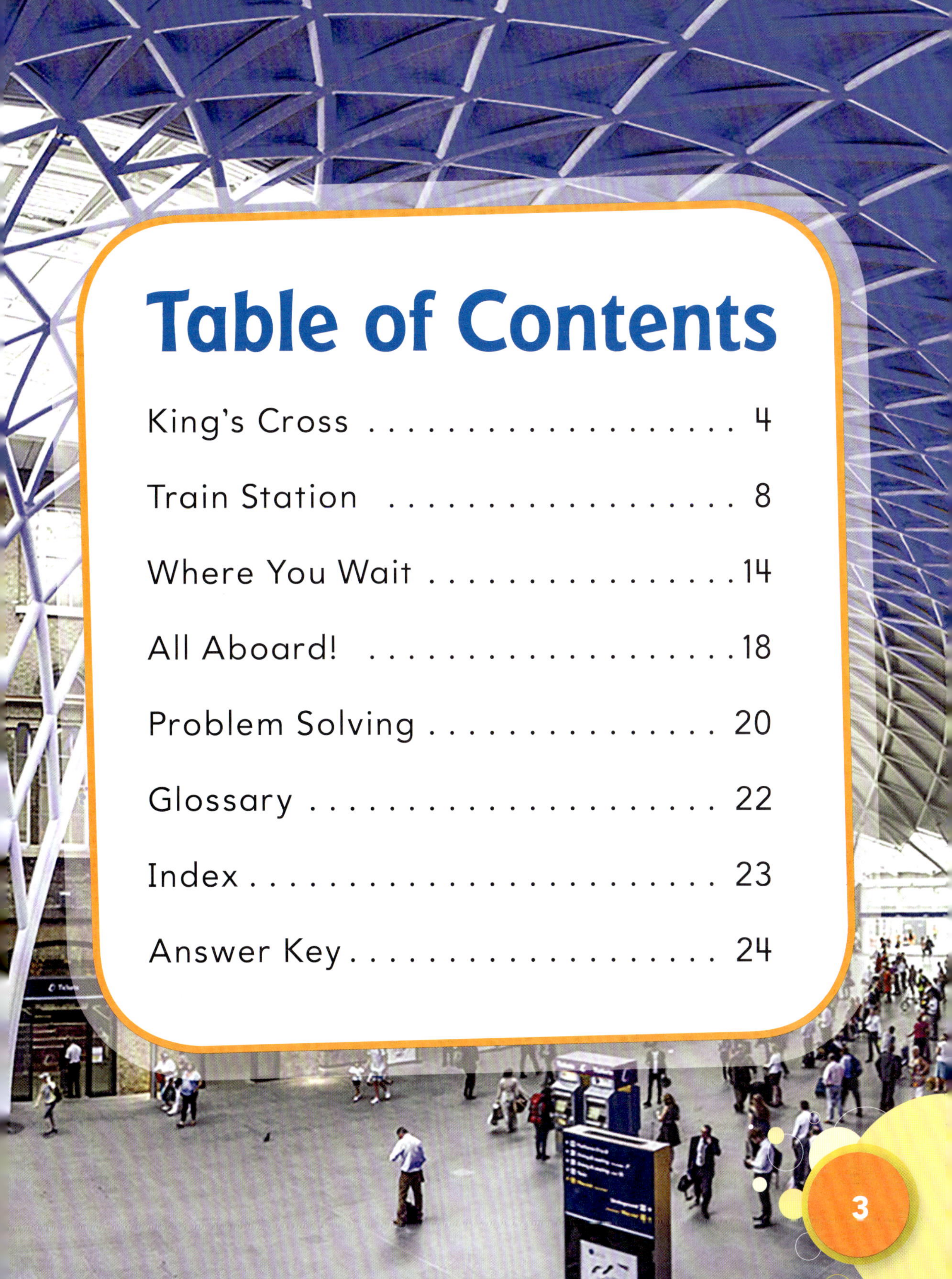

Table of Contents

King's Cross

The world is on the go at King's Cross! It is one of the **busiest** places in London. There are parks, shops, and places to eat. And there is a famous train **station** known around the world.

5

The station was named after a statue called King's Cross. It was built in **honor** of King George.

King George lived long ago.

This statue honored
King George.

Train Station

The train station at King's Cross was built many years ago. Trains came and went from all over. That **hub** still stands. It is the King's Cross Station.

King's Cross Station is a busy place.

Seth designs a train ticket. He wants to make two equal parts.

1. Which design shows two equal parts?

   A.

   C.

   B.

   D.

2. Which math word describes the parts?

   A. halves

   B. twos

   C. quarters

Thousands of people ride the trains. They ride to and from the station each day.

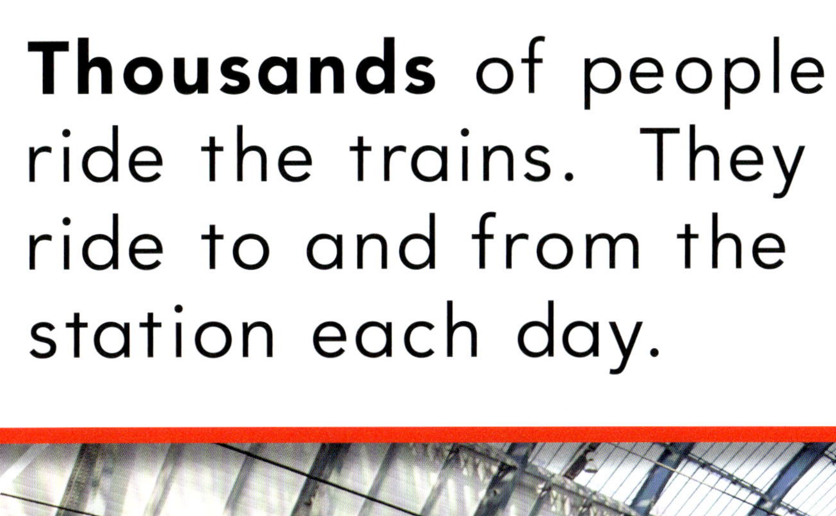

People take trains for different reasons. Some people take trains to get to work.

People take trains to travel, too. They like to visit friends and family.

Four friends sit on a bench to wait for a train. The bench's seat is a rectangle like this one.

Draw rectangles. Show two different ways that four friends can equally share the seat.

Where You Wait

There are 12 **platforms** at King's Cross Station. Each one is where people get on or off trains.

Imagine that a platform floor is a rectangle like this one.

Two classes equally share the floor in the morning. Four classes equally share the same floor in the afternoon.

When do the classes have a larger part of the floor—morning or afternoon? How do you know?

There is a famous platform people like to visit. But it is not real. It is from the Harry Potter books. People pretend a cart in the wall is Harry's cart.

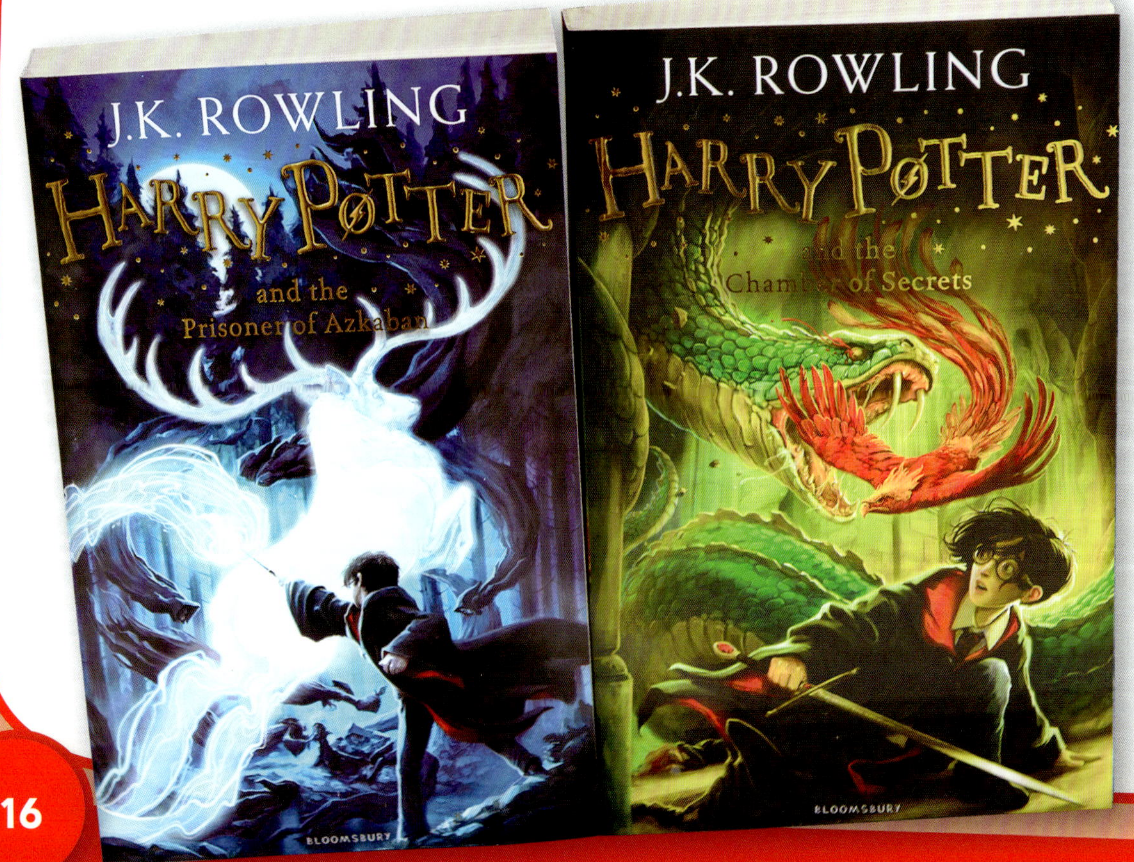

PLATFORM 9¾

All Aboard!

You may want to visit King's Cross Station someday. You will see trains and more. You can pretend you are going to school with Harry Potter. Your trip will be one to remember!

EXPECT
DELAYS
TAXI

Problem Solving

There are restaurants at King's Cross. Friends share sandwiches while waiting for a train. Draw rectangles to solve the problems.

1. Show how Jada and Brady can divide a sandwich into two equal parts.

2. Liam, Jamal, Rose, and Heidi share a sandwich. Show how they can divide a sandwich into four equal parts.

3. Who gets a smaller part of a sandwich—Jada or Liam? How do you know?

Glossary

busiest—with the most activity

honor—respect

hub—very busy place where many trains, planes, or other vehicles meet up

platforms—raised floors where people wait for trains

station—place where trains or buses have regular stops

thousands—any number that is larger than 1,999

Index

Answer Key

Let's Do Math!

page 9:

1. C

2. A

page 13:

Answers will vary. Examples:

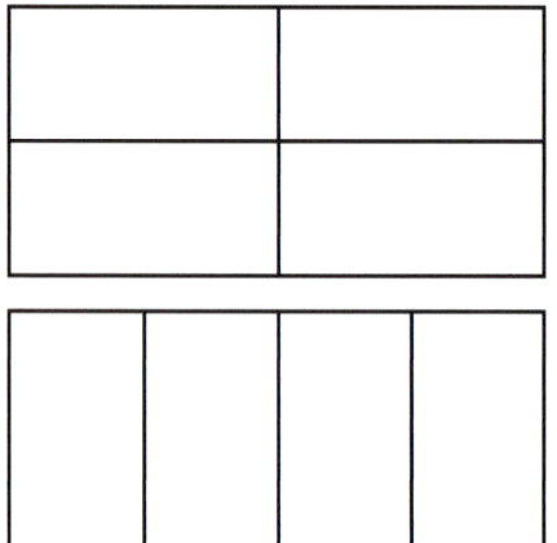

page 15:

morning; halves are larger than fourths of the same floor

Problem Solving

1. Answers will vary. Example:

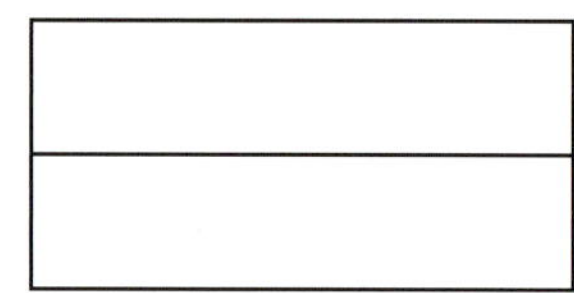

2. Answers will vary. Example:

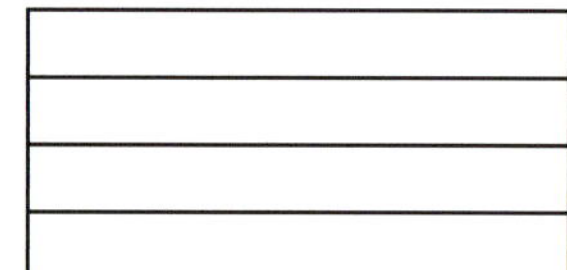

3. Liam; fourths are smaller than halves of the same sandwich